Wilted Whispers

Echoes of Love, Loss and Longing

Shubh Jain

BookLeaf Publishing

India | USA | UK

Dedication

To all Men,

Who carry the weight of unspoken words and
unseen tears,

Who are taught to be pillars but never allowed to
crumble,

Who love deeply in silence and break quietly in
the shadows.

This is for the scars you hide, the battles you
fight,

And the flowers you deserve long before your
final goodbye.

Sit with these words, in the solitude you know so
well,

And feel what the world so often asks you to
forget.

Acknowledgements

'To a certain sunflower I once called mine, thank you for the light you once gave and the shadows you left behind– both taught me how to grow in ways I never imagined'.

To write this book has been both a labour of love and a journey through my own reflections on pain, love and resilience. It would not have been possible without the people who shaped my understanding of the human heart, both through its joys and its sorrows.

To the men who inspired this book, thank you for your quiet strength, your untold stories and your unspoken struggles. This is for you– for the emotions you've hidden, the battles you've fought in silence and the beauty of your humanity that often goes unnoticed.

To the people who have walked in and out of my life, leaving behind lessons I could only learn through heartbreak– thank you. To the sunflower I once called mine, you showed me that growth comes through both light and shadow, and for that, I am grateful.

To my family, thank you for your support in ways I often took for granted. You've been my anchor when the tides of life felt overwhelming, and your love has been a quiet but constant presence in my journey.

To my friends who became my chosen family, thank you for listening to my ramblings, for the late-night conversations that shaped many of these poems and for encouraging me to write even when I doubted myself. Your belief in me gave me the courage to pour my soul onto these pages.

To the men I've never met but whose stories I've witnessed in passing– the father holding back tears, the friend too proud to ask for help, the stranger wearing a smile to hide the ache– you are the heart of this book. Your vulnerability, even when unspoken, is what makes this world a little more human.

Lastly, to the reader holding this book in your hands, thank you for giving these words a home. Whether you are here to explore, to heal or simply to feel, I hope these pages speak to you in a way that reminds you of your own strength, your own softness and the beauty of being unapologetically human.

with gratitude,
Shubh

Preface

Here is a certain kind of silence that men carry. It's not the peaceful kind, but the kind that settles on the chest like an unmoving weight. It lingers in the space between 'I'm fine' and 'I'm breaking'. Society has always expected men to be strong, resilient and stoic – qualities that, while admirable, often come at the cost of emotional vulnerability. Somewhere along the way, the space for men to feel, to express and to heal was stolen, leaving them with hearts full of battles no one sees.

This book, Wilted Whispers, is my offering to that silence. It is an invitation to sit with the emotions you've long buried and let them breathe. It is dedicated to men who have been told that their worth lies in how well they suppress their pain – men who are falling apart but have never been given the space to say so.

Through three carefully woven parts, this book explores the many layers of the masculine experience:

Part One: A Bouquet of Rueful Reflections – A space for the grief, heartbreak and unspoken pain men often carry in silence. These poems capture the weight of loss, the ache of fading friendships and the quiet resilience found in the in-between moments of suffering and survival.

Part Two: What Makes a Good Man – An exploration of strength beyond its conventional definition. These poems question, celebrate and redefine masculinity – not as a set of rigid expectations, but as an evolving journey of integrity, kindness and quiet courage.

Part Three: Whispers of Winter – A soft, nostalgic collection of love, loss and the inevitable seasons of life. Like the crisp air of winter, these poems hold both warmth and melancholy, reminding us that even in endings, there is beauty.

The title, Wilted Whispers, speaks to the stories within these pages. Wilted, because pain, no matter how deeply hidden, leaves its mark. Whispers, because emotions, when long suppressed, have a way of speaking in the quietest moments.

Dandelion

Wishful Scars

You were a dandelion in the wind,
Fragile, fleeting, rooted in nothing–
I made wishes on your existence, each one
whispered
with the foolish hope
that you would stay.

But you scattered.

Your seeds,
like promises,
floated into the air,
their weightlessness
mocking the heaviness
you left in my chest.

I tried to catch them.
To hold onto the pieces
of what you were,
but you were never meant
to stay in one place.

Isn't that the tragedy
of a dandelion?
in its fleeting beauty,
but the leaves behind
only the ghost
of its stem—
a wishful scar
on the earth,
a reminder
of something
I could never keep

and yet,
I loved you still.
Even as the winds
tore you away,
I loved the way
you made me believe
in the impossible
for just a moment.

Rose

Thorns of Memory

You bloomed in my life
like a rose in full blush–
soft petals,
a sweetness that lingered
long after you left.

But I never learned
how to hold you without bleeding.
your thorns were gentle at first,
a whisper against my skin,
until they weren't

Even now,
I trace the scars you left,
tiny constellations
etched into my hands.
They tell stories
of love so fierce
it tore itself apart.

I still smell the rose
when I close my eyes,
feel the phantom sting
of thorns beneath my touch.
you were beautiful,
but beauty is not always kind.

The bloom fades,
the petals fall,
but the thorns–
the thorns
stay forever.

Lotus

Rising from the Mud

I was born in the shadows,
beneath water too murky to reflect the sky.
The weight of the mud clung to me,
pulling me down,
telling me I would never bloom.

But the mud did not know
that it was a teacher.
In its heaviness,
I found strength,
in its darkness,
I found the will to reach for the light.

Every inch I climbed
was a war against the weight,
every breath a defiance
of the silence that tried to drown me.
But I rose,
Petal by petal,
through water that once hid me.

Now, I stand tall,
delicate but untouchable,
floating on the surface of all
that tried to bury me.
I carry the mud with me still–
but not as a burden,
but as proof
that even in the dirtiest places,
something beautiful can grow

Lavender

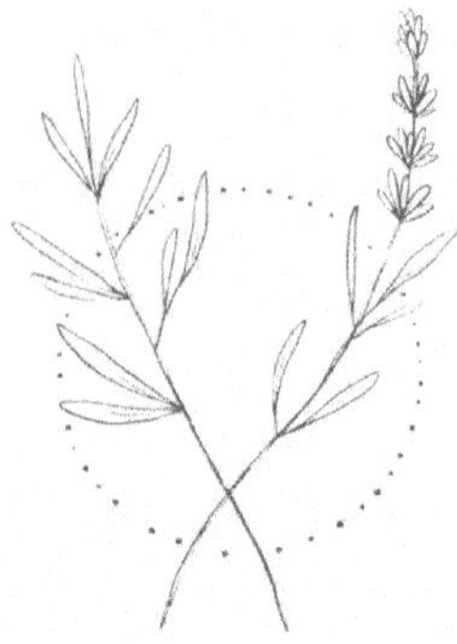

Softened Solitude

I once feared the quiet–
the hollow echo of an empty room,
the stillness that made my thoughts
too loud to ignore.
Loneliness wrapped itself around me
like a cold, unyielding wind.

But then, I found lavender

its scent whispered of peace,
of calm, that does not need
the noise of the world to feel alive

It softened the edges of my solitude,
turning the sharp sting of aloneness
into a tender embrace

Now, I sit in the quiet
and breathe deeply.
I no longer run from myself;
I've learned that the silence
is not my enemy,
but my sanctuary.

Lavender blooms in the stillness,
reminding me that even solitude
can hold the gentlest kind of beauty.

Sunflower

Chasing the Sun

I have always tilted my face towards the light,
chasing something I could never hold.
The Sun, distant and untouchable,
pulls me like a forgotten promise–
a warmth I crave but cannot keep.

Some days, the clouds devoured it,
leaving me searching, aching,
turning in circles for a glow
that had abandoned me.
Still, I kept reaching,
because to stop
felt like surrender.

I am a sunflower.
Even in the darkest hours,
when the sky gives me nothing,
I remember the light.
I turn my face to the memory of it,
believing that someday,
it will return.

And when it does,
I will bloom again–
not because it saved me,
but because I never stopped believing
in the warmth I deserved.

Marigold

A Bloom of Farewells

You stood at the threshold,
a marigold in full bloom–
vivid, golden,
too bright to stay.

Goodbyes were woven
into your petals,
each one a soft reminder
that beauty,
no matter how radiant,
is always fleeting.

I held you in trembling hand,
not ready to let you go,
but marigolds do not wait.
They wither in the grip of hesitation,
leaving their fragrance behind
to haunt the air.

Now, the ache of your absence
lingers like pollen on my skin
I tell myself it was enough–
to see you bloom,
to feel your light.

But some farewells
are not meant to heal.
they are meant to teach us
how to carry the ache,
like pressed flowers in a book,
fragile but eternal.

Tulip

Fleeting Spring

You came with the first warmth of spring,
soft and sudden,
like a whisper of joy
after a long winter.

For a moment,
the world felt lighter–
your colours painting my days
in hues I had forgotten existed.
You were fragile, yes,
but in your fragility,
I found hope

and then,
as quickly as you bloomed,
you began to fade.
petals fell, one by one
and I tried to catch them,
to hold onto the brightness
before it slipped away.

But tulips are not forever
They are meant to teach us
that happiness, like spring,
is fleeting

and yet,
in their short-lived beauty, they remind us to
cherish–
not what stays,
but blossoms,
even if only for a moment.

Orchid

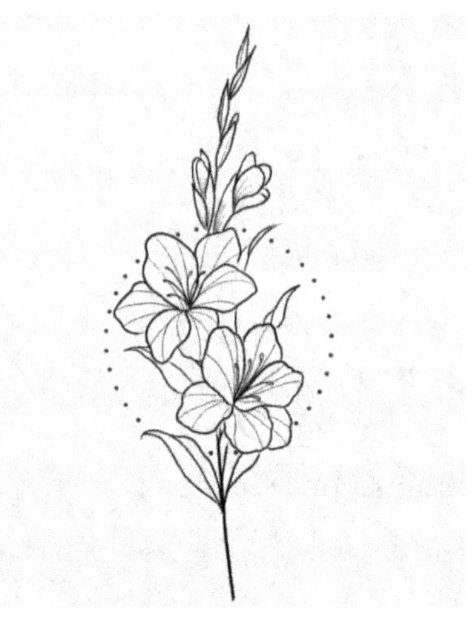

Fragile Elegance

You stood quietly in the corner,
delicate and unassuming,
yet impossible to ignore.
An Orchid's beauty
does not shout;
it whispers,
soft as a secret
waiting to be heard.

Your petals looked fragile,
like they could shatter
under the weight of a single breath.
But beneath that fragility
was a quiet strength–
roots gripping tightly
to what nourished you,
refusing to let go.

I saw myself in you;
vulnerable but enduring
soft yet unyielding,
You taught me
that strength is not always loud,
and survival
does not have to be violent

Sometimes,
It's enough to simply bloom,
even if the world
only sees your softness
and not the battles you fought
to grow

Jasmine

Night's Confessions

The jasmine blooms
when the world is quiet,
its fragrance a confession
carried on the night air,
meant only for the moon.

In its delicate scent,
there are whispers of secrets—
loves unspoken,
tears unseen,
dreams left to wither
beneath the weight of dawn.

Under the watchful gaze
of silver light,
I speak to the jasmine.
my regrets,
the shadows that follow me.
it listens,
never asking for more.

There's a heaviness in the stillness,
a truth too raw
to exist in daylight.
but here,
in the safety of the night,
I let it breathe.

By morning
the jasmine fades
its confession carried away
on the first breeze.
but the moon remembers,
and so do I.

Carnation

Fraying Edges

We were never perfect,
but we held on anyway,
threads of us tangled tightly
against the pull of time.
You were the carnation
I thought would last forever–
soft, familiar,
rooted in love
I didn't know how to let go.

But love, like fabric
can wear thin.
The edges of us began to fray,
quietly at first,
until one day
we unravelled

Even as the threads fell away,
I couldn't hate you.
You left behind something warm—
memories stitched with laughter,
moments of tenderness
that still bloom in the quiet.

Now, I carry what's left of us,
a bittersweet comfort
pressed between pages of who we were.
We didn't stay whole.
and perhaps,
that's enough

Peony

The Weight of Beauty

You stood there, radiant,
a peony in full bloom,
each petal soft as silk,
each curve a masterpiece.
The world admired you,
awed by your grace,
but no one asked
what it costs you to bloom.

They didn't see the strain
of holding yourself together,
the weight of perfection
pressed upon your fragile stem.
They saw the beauty,
but not the storm beneath–
the roots tangled in unseen soil,
the silent cracks in your foundation.

You smiled,
even as the wind tore at your edges,
even as your petals grew heavy
with the burden of their own allure.
To be beautiful,
they said
is to be loved
but you learned
that beauty often comes
with the loneliness
of being seen
but never known.

and yet,
you kept blooming.
Not for them

but for yourself—
to prove that even under the weight,
you could carry the sky
and still be soft.

Bluebell

Essence of Youth

There was a time
when life felt endless,
each day soft and weightless
like a bluebell swaying
in a gentle breeze.

The laughter was unfiltered,
the tears easily dried.
The world was smaller then,
but somehow brighter,
painted colours
I can't seem to find any more.

Now, I walk through fields
of my memories
searching for that fleeting scent
of innocence,
the echoes of laughter
that once filled my lungs.

But the bluebells are gone,
their petals scattered
by the winds of time.
What remains
is the ache of knowing
I can never return,
and the sweetness of having
once been there.

Youth is a flower
that blooms only once,
its beauty fleeting,
but its roots forever buried
in the soil of who we become

Chrysanthemum

Wilted Promises

You spoke in blooms,
your words like petals,
soft and full of colour,
each one a promise
I cradled in my hands

But petals are fragile things.
Promises, even more so.
And one by one,
they withered,
turning brittle under the weight
of time and truth.

I tried to hold on,
but the stems you left me
were hollow,
their roots too shallow
to sustain what you'd sown.
The garden of us
became a graveyard
of wilted words.

Still, I can't forget the way you bloomed,
even if it was fleeting.
I can't hate the beauty
that once was,
even if it left behind
only dried petals
and broken stems.

Chrysanthemums don't last forever,
but their memory lingers–
a ghost of promises
that never found their spring.

Cherry Blossom

A Season of Letting Go

You arrived with the gentleness
of a cherry blossom in spring,
your presence fleeting,
your beauty undeniable.
For a moment,
I forgot that you would fall.

The petals began to drift,
softly, silently,
carried by a wind
I could not control.
I tried to catch them,
tried to hold on
what was never mine to keep

But blossoms are meant to fall.
They teach us that even the most beautiful
things
are not promised forever–
that lover, like spring,
is borrowed time.

Now, I stand beneath the empty branches,
the ground carpeted in what you left behind.
it aches to let go,
but there is peace in the release–
in knowing that your beauty
was not diminished
but its importance.

Some things cannot stay,
but their memory lingers,
soft petals,
fragile as the wind.

Iris

Whispers of Hope

It wasn't grand,
the way you gave me light.
it wasn't a sunbeam
breaking through clouds,
but a flicker,
soft as steady,
like the glow of an iris
in the first breath of spring.

You didn't speak in loud declarations.
Your kindness was quiet,
a hand brushing mine
when I couldn't see the path ahead,
a word spoken softly
when the world felt too loud.

I learned, through you,
that hope doesn't always roar
Sometimes it whispers,
nudging us forward
in the smallest of ways.

Your light taught me
to search for the gentle moments—
a sunrise tucked into a stranger's smile,
a spark hidden in the touch
of someone who believes
when you cannot.

An iris blooms quietly,
without demand,
yet its beauty is enough
to remind me
that faith need not be loud
only present.

Poppy

Fields of Forgotten Pain

Grief is a poppy field,
its bloom bright and bold,
masking the ache that lies beneath the soil.
Time scatters seeds,
and we think we've moved on,
but the roots remain,
hidden,
waiting to bloom again.

I told myself the pain had faded,
but lingers in quiet moments–
the silence of a sunset,
the whisper of a familiar song.

like the poppy, grief doesn't disappear;
it grows in the cracks of memory,
softly reminding me
of what I've lost

I walk through the field,
the colours vivid,
and I wonder–
or is it sorrow disguised
as something I can bear?

Grief doesn't forget.
it wears the mask of time,
but beneath the petals,
it is still there,
rooted deep,
waiting for me
to remember.

Hibiscus

Flames of Desire

You came to me like fire,
a hibiscus in full bloom,
red and wild,
your passion consuming
everything in its path.
I held you close,
knowing the burn was inevitable,
but craving the heat
all the same.

You were more than a love;
you were hunger,
a storm that ignited
every corner of my being.
Your touch left scars,
but I wore them like badges,
proof of the inferno
We created together.

When the flames finally dimmed,
I stood among the ashes,
the echoes of your bloom
still burning in my veins.
You left behind nothing soft,
only embers that smoulder,
reminding me of a love
too fierce to survive.

The hibiscus taught me this:
passion is beautiful,
but it consumes.
And even as it leaves you hollow,
you'll find yourself longing
for the fire once more.

Magnolia

Roots of Resilience

You do not see the roots
when a magnolia blooms.
You only see the flowers,
delicate and proud,
a quiet triumph against the sky.
But beneath the earth,
the story is written in silence–
roots tangled and deep,
anchored in soil that has known storms.

I am like the magnolia.
My strength does not shout,
but it is there,
buried in the lessons of where I began,
in the hands that held me,
the voices that shaped me,
the struggles that tested me.

I've bent in the wind,
I've weathered the rain,
but I have not broken.
Each storm only forced my roots
to dig deeper,
finding resilience
in the very ground that tried to bury me.

The magnolia blooms
not because it has forgotten the storms,
but because it has survived them.
and so do I,
carrying my foundation
as both a burden and a gift,
a testament to where I've been
and the strength that brought me here.

Daisy

Silent Summers

There was a time
when joy came quietly,
like the soft sway of daisies
beneath a summer sky.
the days were endless,
painted in sunlight and laughter,
yet so delicate
that we didn't realise
they were slipping away.

We spoke in whispers,
shared smiles that lingered,
never thinking to hold tighter–
Why would we?
It felt like the warmth would stay forever.

But summers fade,
and daisies wilt.
Now, I sit in the silence they left behind,
tracing the outlines of those memories,
their petals pressed between
the pages of my mind.

It's not the grand moments I miss,
but the small ones–
the laughter in the shade of trees,
the simplicity of being happy
without knowing why.

The daisies may have withered,
but their roots remain,
buried deep,
quietly reminding me
of the summers we never thought
would end.

Wildflower

Unbridled Spirit

You grew where no one thought you could,
among the cracks in the earth,
untamed,
unclaimed.
The world called you wild,
but you called yourself free.

No garden walls could hold you,
no hands could shape your bloom.
You were never meant
to fit into rows or rules–
you were chaos and beauty,
a spirit untethered
to anyone's design.

The wind carried you,
and you followed,
your roots reaching not for approval,
but for the promise of the unknown.
Every petal told a story of a rebellion,
of choosing to grow
on your own terms.

They asked why you refused to conform,
why you stood apart from their order.
You only smiled,
because they could never understand
the joy of being
everything the world told you not to be.

A wildflower blooms
not for the praise of others,
but for the sheer delight
of existing exactly as it is
free, unbridled
and unapologetically itself.

Forget me Not

Fragments Forever

You left,
but pieces of you stayed
small, quiet fragments
woven into the fabric of my days.
A laugh that echoes
in the stillness of the morning,
a touch I feel
when no one is near.

Time hasn't erased you.
it only softens the edges,
like sunlight through a dusty window,
blurred but still there.
Some moments remain untouched,
frozen in the amber of memory,
refusing to fade
no matter how far I walk from you.

I didn't ask for this
to carry you with me,

but here you are,
in the scent of rain,
in the songs I can't bear to play.
You are everywhere
and nowhere,
a ghost of love that lingers.

The forget-me-not blooms
with quiet defiance,
its roots tangled in the past.
And like the flower,
I hold onto the pieces of us
not because I can't let go,
but because some memories are meant to stay
forever.

Part 2:

What makes a good man?

Be the Calm

when the world screams
its chaos into your soul
stand still–
let their panic
pass through you like wind
through an ancient tree.
do not catch fire
from their fear,
hold the quiet
in your chest.
you are the mountain,
you are the ocean.
They are only storms.
some will crumble.
some will drown.
but you–
you will shine,
a steady star,
lighting the way home.

Be the Quiet Flame

trust the fire in your chest—
it knows the way.
but do not let it burn so bright
that it drowns the stars around you.
even the sun
listens to the whispers of the moon.
your strength is not diminished
by another's light.
it is deepened

by the wisdom you gather,
like rivers shaping stone.
walk boldly,
but bow with grace.
the tallest tree
still bends to the wind,
for humility
is the bridge between knowing yourself
and learning from the world.

Be the unshaken flame

when the world
hurls its noise at you,
hold your silence close.
patience is not surrender–
it is the art of standing still
while chaos wears itself thin.
let their dishonesty
fall like leaves in autumn,
while you remain
the rooted tree,
untouched by their decay.
do not meet hatred
with fire.
rise above,
your integrity
a lantern that needs no match.
the earth does not strain
to prove its strength–
it simply endures,
unmoved,
until time
sets all things right.

Trust the Sky and Soil

dream wildly—
let your thoughts
touch the edge of the sky,
but do not forget
the ground beneath your feet.

even the tallest tree
must root itself in the earth
to keep from falling.
your mind is a vast ocean,
your ideas, the waves—
but if you chase each one,
you will never reach the shore.
imagine freely,
think deeply,
but walk forward
with steady steps.
the stars are beautiful,
but you were meant
to live here—
with the sun on your face
and the earth in your hands.

Go Beyond the Rise and Fall

they will cheer for you
when you rise,
they will turn away
when you fall.
do not mistake applause
for truth,
nor silence for failure.
success is a passing breeze,
failure a fading storm–
neither is the air
that keeps you breathing.
walk steady,
whether the road is gold
or gravel.
you are not the heights you reach,
nor the depths you sink to–
you are the one
who keeps walking.

Rise Again

they will take from you
what you built with bare hands
they will turn their backs
when you need them most
but you–
you are not what is lost
you are what remains
the seed does not weep
when the storm takes its leaves
it digs deeper
into the earth
and begins again
you may have nothing
but your breath
but that is enough
to take the next step
rise again–
not because the world is kind
but because you are unbreakable

Leap Without Fear

do not fear the fall
fear the life
where you never jump
the bird does not ask
if the branch will hold–
it simply spreads its wings
you will lose
you will stumble
but each step forward
is still a step forward
the sun sets without regret
knowing it will rise again
so take the risk
fall if you must
but always–
rise with the dawn

Tame the Fire Within

when your body aches
when your mind begs to stop
when the road stretches too far
and your strength feels like a whisper—
keep walking.
you were not made
to break at the first storm
you were made to bend,
to endure,
to rise.
the sun does not refuse to shine
because the night was long
nor does the river stop flowing
because the rocks stand in its way.
even when you have nothing left
there is still something within you
a quiet flame
that refuses to die—
let it guide you forward.

Remember your Roots
and Wings

no matter how high
you rise
remember the earth
that once cradled your steps
the wind does not ask
if the tree is mighty or small
it brushes against both
just the same
a throne means nothing
if you forget
how to sit beside the weary
a crown is weightless
if it rests on a hollow heart
be the one
who greets kings and beggars alike

with the same open hands
for true greatness
is not in how high you stand
but in how deeply you bow

No Time to Waste

do not wait
for the perfect moment–
this one is already slipping away
the sun does not pause
to ask if the sky is ready
it simply rises
your hands are not empty
they hold the seconds
that could build empires
or be lost like sand in the wind
plant the seed now
write the words now
love now–
before time reminds you
that it never waits

More Than a King

when the world crumbles
beneath your feet
stand tall–
not with pride,
but with quiet strength
walk with kings
but never forget
the language of the common man
hold power lightly
but honour deeply
meet triumph and disaster
as twin impostors–
smiling at both,
knowing neither
define you
when your hands are empty
let your heart remain full

when all is lost
keep faith
for a man is not measured
by what he gains

but by what he refuses to lose
and when you have given
all that you are–
your courage, your patience,
your wisdom, your grace–
you will find
that you have not just won the world
but mastered yourself

The search for happiness

I climbed the highest mountain
thinking happiness lived in the sky
I wandered the deepest valley
believing it waited in the distance
but in my searching
I found only echoes—
whispers of a truth
I had long forgotten
happiness was never hiding
it was always near—
in the laughter of a friend
the warmth of a hand in mine
the quiet comfort of solitude
the freedom in being myself
and letting others be who they are
I searched the world
only to find
that joy was not a treasure to seek
but a light I carried all along

Whispers of Winter

The Needle

Grief is a needle
tucked into the pocket of our days.
We walk with it,
unnoticed, unbothered,
until the fabric shifts–
a memory,
a glance,
a scent of what was lost.
And there it is,
piercing flesh,
reminding us that healing
is not the absence of pain,
but the quiet courage
to carry the needle
and still move forward.

The Feast We Deserve

we take crumbs from the table
and call it a feast
because no one told us
we were deserving of more
we plant ourselves in shallow soil
wondering why we never bloom
but growth demands belief
in a worth we've yet to claim
you are not meant for scraps
or for wilted gardens
you are the sun, the rain
the fire that ignites forests
dare to believe

you are worthy of the world
and watch as it bends
to your unrelenting light

Give and take

I know my kindness hurts me
like a blade hidden in soft petals,
but I will continue to choose–
not because I am naive,
not because I seek to be saved,
but because my actions define me.
I am not the storm that strikes
nor the fire that consumes;
I am the steady river,
cutting through stone,
with gentleness
and resolve.
Let others mistake my mercy for weakness,
let the world think me a fool.
I will water the barren earth
with the best of myself,
even if it leaves me parched.
For in the end,
I am not what they take from me–
I am what I give.

Whispers of the Mountains

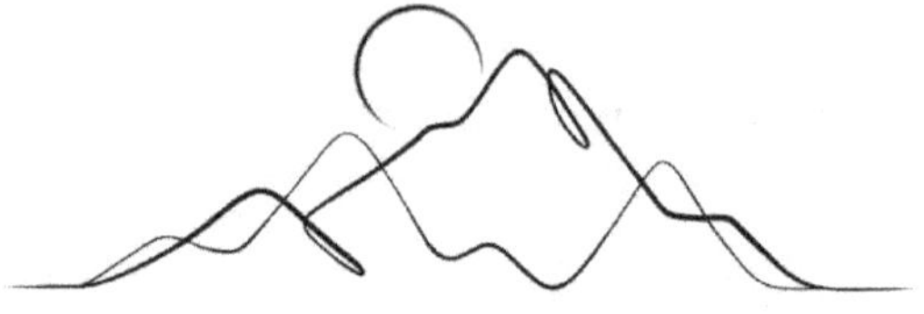

I went to the mountains
To find silence,
But they spoke louder
Than my fears–
Each peak, a lesson
Etched in ice and stone.
The air was thin,
Yet my thoughts
were heavier than ever.
Each step reminded me
That progress
Is not measured in leaps
But in breaths taken
One at a time.
The path was not mine to conquer
But to surrender to–

To learn that the journey
Is not about the journey
Is not about the summit
But the strength found
In the climb
I learned that failure
Is not the absence of reaching,
But the refusal to rise again.
The cold taught me warmth,
The height taught me humility,
And the vastness taught me
How small I truly am–
And yet,
How infinite my spirit can be.
The mountains whispered–
You are both the storm
And the stillness.
Trust the climb,
For it is you unfolding.

The Mirror of Healing

the purpose of love
is not to complete us
but to crack us open
how can wounds heal
if they are hidden away?
how can the light enter
if we deny the fracture?
the ego whispers–
stay veiled, stay safe
for honesty might
turn beauty into burden
and love might leave
but hear this:
growth waits on the other side
of fear's fragile gate
without growth, love wilts
boredom's quiet death
settling in the stillness
the perfect partner?
a mirage of the mind
a smoke screen to keep us
from gazing inward

true healing begins
when we stop searching
for perfection in another
and find the holy within ourselves
show yourself–
not to keep love
but to become it.

If She Loves You Now

she is not untouched soil
nor an unbroken wave
she has been the sky
for storms that have passed
but if she loves you now—
her heart in your hands
like a trembling bird
what else is there to seek?
do not ask for her past
to vanish like smoke
nor for her future
to belong to you alone
her love is not perfect
it is real
and if she places it at your feet
let that be enough
the moon has scars
yet its light
still moves the tides

Shattered and Seen

these tears are not for you
but for the dream I cradled
the gentle illusion
of who I thought you were
you were a mirage
a tender shape carved
by my own longing
and when the truth stepped forward
it was not you who broke me
but my own reflection
now I see you–
not as I wished
but as you are
and though it stings
there is freedom in the fracture
for in the ruin of delusion
there is the birth of clarity

and in seeing you truly
I begin to find myself.

The Weight of Silence

I placed a weight on your shoulders
without a word,
expecting you to know
the shape of my longing.
how could you?
I carried the map in my mind,
never showing you the way
yet blaming you for getting lost.
unspoken desires
are seeds of quiet resentment–
growing roots deep in the dark
until they crack the foundation.
love cannot bloom
where silence takes root.
to be known,
we must first be brave enough
to speak.

The Cost of Silence

you asked nothing of me–
but in your quiet eyes
I saw the weight of
a thousand unsaid words.
I stumbled blindly
through your unspoken labyrinth,
tripping over expectations
I could not see.
and when the cracks appeared,
you called them my doing.
but how could I meet a need
you never let me hold?
love is not a guessing game.
it is a bridge built together–

yet you left me standing alone
on the edge of silence.

When It Arrives

the universe is not cruel–
it is a weaver,
threading moments together
with infinite care.
what feels like waiting
is not stillness,
but quiet preparation.
it is clearing the path,
aligning the stars,
steadying the earth beneath your feet,
so that when it arrives
it does not slip away.
trust the hands
that hold the threads.
what is meant for you
is not late–
it is being built to stay

What Love Remains

do you love the flame
or the warmth it gives?
the way it lights your path
or how it dances for your eyes?
love is not proven
in the glow of presence,
but in the shadow
left behind.
when the thrill fades,
when the mirror of ego cracks,
does your heart still whisper
their name in prayer?
true love lingers–
not for what they bring
but for who they are,
even when their light
no longer shines for you.
to love someone

when they are nothing to you
is the only love
that is everything

Behind the Grip

control is the fist clenched tight
around the fragile stem of fear—
not to crush it,
but to keep it from slipping away.
we do not grip
without reason.
we hold on
because the unknown whispers
its terrible promises.
do not ask the hand to let go
ask instead
what it trembles to lose.
the heart behind control
is not cruel—
it is afraid.
and when fear is seen,
the grip softens.

The Voices of Letting Go

grief whispers–
I miss them.
it hurts.
its voice is soft,
but it carves deep.
anger shouts–
this isn't fair!
it shakes the walls
but cannot rebuild them.
regret sighs–
I wish I had done more,
its weight presses
but changes nothing.
confusion whispers–
why did it end?
its echo lingers
without answers.
and then acceptance–
quiet and steady–

replies,
not every love is meant to last.

hope nudges softly—
maybe this ending
is a beginning,
and suddenly,
the heart begins
to believe.

When Convincing
Becomes the Love

love does not beg
to be believed.
it settles into the soul
like rain sinking into the earth.
if you spend more time
building reasons in your mind
than feeling truth in your heart,
you already know.
love that fits
does not demand convincing–
it simply is.
but the heart,
so afraid of empty hands,
holds on to the weight
of what it knows is not right.
listen–
if you must persuade yourself,
it is not love.
it is fear wearing its mask.

The Balance of Love

giving more than you have
is not love—
it is the quiet breaking
of your own spirit.
self-betrayal wears
the mask of devotion,
but behind it
is a heart that whispers
I am empty.
love is not a sacrifice
that leaves one starving.
it is a river
that flows between two souls,
nourishing both.
a healthy love
does not drain,
it sustains.
it grows in the light
of mutual care.
to pour from an empty cup
is not love—
it is forgetting

that you, too,
are worthy of being filled.

Undiluted

I have no desire
to be for everyone–
to shape myself
into something easy to swallow.
sometimes my truth
will burn like whiskey,
leaving a fire in its wake.
sometimes it will soothe
like nectar,
sweet on the tongue.
but I will never

pour myself into smaller cups,
nor water down my essence
to fit someone's palate.
I am not here
to be consumed–
I am here
to be known,
exactly as I am.

Silence of Solitude

in the quiet
I learned
to hold myself
the way I wanted others to
solitude showed me
the parts of my soul
I was too afraid to see
and the courage
to love them anyway
silence whispered
you are not broken
you are becoming
listen carefully
to the lessons within
only when I embraced the stillness
did I realise
the noise was never home

What Do You Mean by Love

Do you call it love
when it sways like the wind,
sometimes a storm,
sometimes a whisper?
Is it the flame
that burns steady and warm,
or the fire
that consumes without mercy?
Love is not the word
you say with your lips,
but the truth
you carve into the soul.
It is not possession,
nor fleeting desire–
it is the sun rising within,
giving light even in shadow.

Some People Save You

they do not arrive
with roaring sirens
or heroic leaps into flames–
they save you
in the silence.
a hand on your shoulder
when words
can't hold you steady.
a look that says
I see your pain
and I am here.
they save you
in the ordinary–

a cup of tea on a hard day,
a gentle laugh
when the world feels too loud.
no one writes stories
about those
who save you quietly,
but they are the ones
who keep your heart
beating.

For the Right One

you could shine
like the brightest star
and still
their eyes will wander
if they are not meant for you.
but stumble
in your darkest hour
and the right one
will reach for your hand
like they were born to hold it.
it is not your worth
that falters–
it is their ability
to see it.
the right one
will love you
not because you are perfect,
but because even in your chaos
you are enough.

Not Written for You

it can rest
in the palm of your hands—
soft, warm,
close enough to feel
its breath on your skin.
yet it slips,
a quiet truth
you cannot hold,

a story
that was never yours to tell.
some things
arrive to teach you
how to let go—
not every touch
is meant to stay.
what isn't written for you
will leave
no matter
how tightly you hold on.

If You Love Them

they say
if you love them, let them go
but they do not know
the weight of a soul
that feels like home.
why should I surrender
to the storms of doubt?
why let go of a love
that blooms in the cracks
of imperfection?
they say
there will be others
as if hearts are replaceable
as if every glance
holds the same gravity.
if you love them
never let them go.
this is a battle
worth every scar—
to lose them
is to spend a lifetime
searching for what
can never be found again.

React or Respond

when you react

it is the wound speaking–
the anger, the fear,
the trembling hands
of a younger version of you.
it is the shadow
of your insecurities,
the echo of pain
still begging to be heard.
but when you respond
it is the strength
of who you are becoming–
a reflection of the calm
you fought so hard to find.
one shows the scars
that still ache.
the other,
the light
you've learned to carry.

Strong at the Broken Places

the world has a way
of finding your cracks–
pressing into them
until you shatter.
it leaves you in pieces,
scattered,
aching to be whole
once more.
but when you rise,
you are no longer the same.
each fracture
now holds a story,
each scar
a lesson in resilience.
broken is not the end.
it is where you discover
how strong
you can truly become.

They Know

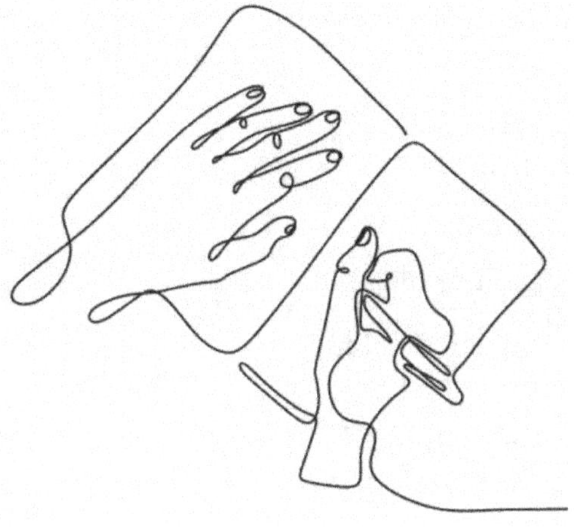

the person who hurt you
does not need to be told–
they carry the weight
of their choice
in silence.
you thought
they never would,
that love
would guard you like a shield.
but love, too,
can falter.
their betrayal

was not an accident.
it was a decision
made in the moment
you believed
they were incapable of it.
your healing
will not come
from their apology–
but from the strength
to accept
what they chose
and walk away whole.

Homeless

when you build a home
in the heart of another,
you hand them the key
to your shelter.
their storms
become your ruin,
their leaving
your collapse.
no one warns you
that love
should be an exchange–
not a surrender
of every wall
you've ever built.
build your home
inside yourself,

so no one
can leave you homeless again.

The Weight of
Mountains

these mountains
that bend your back,
pressing their weight
into your soul,
were never meant
to be carried.
you were meant
to climb them,
to feel the earth
beneath your hands,
to reach the summit
and leave the burden behind.
but you hold them still,
as if bearing their weight
proves your worth.
let them go—
step forward,
the climb
is where your freedom lives.

The Fear of Falling

you hesitate at the edge,
not because the leap
is too great–
but because you have seen
how love can unravel,
how it crumbles
when the wind changes.
you fear the heights
of their embrace,
because you know
the ground waits below.
but love is not
a promise of forever.

it is a risk
you take anyway,
trusting the fall
to teach you
how to rise.

The Barriers

your task
is not to chase love
as if it is a fleeting shadow,
nor to beg the universe
to deliver it to your door.
your task
is to turn inward,
to find the walls
you have built
brick by brick,
to keep love out.
fear,
disappointment,
the ghosts of what was–
these are the barriers
you must tear down.
for love is not hidden,
it is waiting–
patiently–
on the other side
of the walls
you have created.

www.ingramcontent.com/pod-product-compliance
Lightning Source LLC
LaVergne TN
LVHW050915200726
843508LV00011B/2199